Wisdom @Work

Insights for the 21st Century

Worklife Success

JoAnn R. Corley

Wisdom @ Work – Insights for the 21st Century Worklife Success

Cover design: CreateSpace

Printer: CreateSpace

Back Cover Photo: JoAnn R. Corley

Printed in the USA

Library of Congress Cataloging-in-publication Data available upon request

ISBN- 1452893381

ωisdom

The power of true and right discernment

... the ability to see

Attaining wisdom in ancient cultures was a life-long pursuit relegated to a select few. Today anyone can choose to pursue wisdom.

I believe we all want wisdom and that our world runs more smoothly when we use it. I also believe that we all have it...to one degree or another... our own unique brand and that some choose to use it more than others.

As a career and business management coach I feel one place where more wisdom could be applied is in our workplace. That's why I decided to create this "book of wisdom" within the framework of our work life.

In **Wisdom@Work – Insights for the 21**st **Century Worklife Success**, you'll find many words of wisdom I've coined, along with words from others that have inspired and challenged me. They carry with them critical themes necessary to be successful both personally and professionally.

Read slowly, listen closely and allow yourself to open up to the impressions you're feeling as they lift off the pages and into your heart, mind, and spirit - so simply stated yet so powerful in impact.

Space was intentionally left beneath each statement for you to write your own reflections....the wisdom that is being stirred within you. Write your thoughts down and share them with others.

Let this book, move you toward and awaken within you your own valuable, needed unique wisdom!

It is my hope that through these shared experiences our professional community can be strengthened and encouraged toward respect and prosperity!

Your fellow sojourner,

JoAnn

1. Do not confuse activity for achievement.

   John Wooden

2. You must manage your "on-line" brand - do an open search on your name at least every six months.

3. Use social networking, particularly to build a professional brand and network outside your company.

4. The quality of who you are matters more than what you know.

5. You need to be skilled at nurturing and
maintaining a respectful working
rapport.

6. You are a part of a global economy.

7. Knowing the fundamentals of software is no longer an option. You must at least know Word, Excel, and Powerpoint.

8. Build and maintain a personal/professional portfolio.

9. For career success you must not only manage your own performance, but manage the *perception* of your performance as well.

10. Create your own definition of success, if not, you'll be following someone else's.

11. You will never get paid for how much you are really worth.

12. Know that leadership is a behavior, not necessarily a title.

13. Employees give their managers too much power over them.

14. A healthy relationship is an equal balance of power.

15. Bosses need to be managed too.

16. People hire you for your perceived skill. They keep you for who you are.

17. Skill is not something you know how to do; it's something you know how to do *well*.

18. In the 21st century workplace a job
description is really a road map to the
journey of outcomes. Allow some detours.

19. Use discretion with what you post on-line.

20. It takes more emotional intelligence than ever to be an effective professional.

21. Being too tied to technology for long
periods of time can actually lower your I.Q.

22. Great leadership in small groups is needed now more than ever.

23. Don't ever let a manager or supervisor suppress a gut feeling or intuitive nudging that when acted upon could positively impact you, your team members, or the greater good.

24. Have your own voice – or else
someone will talk for you.

25. If you don't consider yourself a leader in some way, you will undermine your talent.

26. Employees become too "co-dependent" on their companies. A company is not your momma and daddy.

27. Keep learning to build a meaningful knowledge base.

28. Keep evolving.

29. Troubled people cause trouble.

30. Keep developing new skills.

31. You must first be your own coach.

32. Find your "juice."

33. Be clear about your values – what really matters to you in work and life.

34. Respect colleagues even when they don't deserve it. Your ability to show respect is more about you than them.

35. What you do and what you don't do create a ripple effect every day.

36. Problem solving, not problem evaluating is an essential skill.

37. Everyone is creative.

38. A lack of emotional maturity is the #1 cause of difficult and disruptive behavior in the workplace.

39. Hurting people hurt people.

40. Become skilled at managing your own
stress.

41. Know your hot points – volunteer for a "time out" when needed.

42. One of the greatest psychological needs that any human has is the need to feel heard. – Listening is a needed professional skill.

43. Focus on a few things and do them exceptionally well.

44. We all get results – it's just a matter of if it's the ones we really wanted or intended.

45. Personal power trumps positional
    power every single time.

46. Budget for your own professional learning and development. If your company pays for some, consider yourself lucky.

47. Financial management is also a matter of career management. Don't ever get stuck working in a place where abuse is tolerated or your health on any level is compromised and you can't leave.

48. People prefer to do business with people they like.

49. Always have an exit strategy, even if it takes a while to execute.

50. Always have an updated resume –
    keep it current.

51. Learn to quantify your work activities with numbers and percentages.

52. Remember the Law of Money: Undervalue what you do, and the world undervalues who you are. *Suze Orman*

.

53. Hearing is not the same as learning.

54. It takes courage to grow up to be who you really are.

55. Just because you told them, doesn't mean they heard it.

56. Listen to the words – watch the behavior. Always believe the behavior.

57. Practice self-truth – When you say, "That was out of character for me." Realize and admit – if it showed up...it was you.

58. Be able to accept criticism even when it's not delivered in the best way.

59. Learn to use the power of silence.

60. Not everything said, requires a response.

61. You are responsible for your own destiny – not your company.

62. Send hand written notes and cards – that speak volumes.

63. Most people spend more time planning their retirement than they do planning their career. Take time to plan your career.

64. The average adult will have at least 2-3 careers in their lifetime.

65. Be willing to reinvent yourself.

66. Create the balance of taking yourself
seriously – then again, not taking yourself
so seriously.

67. Respect differences.

68. We see the world as we are, not
necessarily as it is.

69. Model the behavior you wish everyone else had – be the example.

70. Be believable.

71. Say what you mean and mean what you say.

72. We train people how to treat us.

73. What people tolerate says a lot about who they are.

74. Always be an independent thinker.

75. Be capable of engaging in robust disagreement without taking it personally.

76. Manage your conformity.

77. Know that not everyone really wants a better life or wants to do a great job.

78. We are the sum total of our conditioning to date.

79. There is always a reason behind a behavior.

80. Sometimes we enable bad behavior unintentionally.

81. Be coachable.

82. Leave the past where it is, just bring the lessons learned forward.

83. Be a leader and a follower.

84. Busy doesn't necessarily mean
    productive.

85. Unhealthy people with power are dangerous.

86. People lie.

87. Develop emotional muscles.

88. Self-interest and self-preservation are
    key drivers in most human behavior.

89. Action brings clarity.

90. Words create reality.

91. Negative stress is created not so much by the event, but by the story we give it.

92. The irony of experience – it can block
innovative thinking.

93. Admit your mistakes quickly...offer a solution quicker.

94. To grow – you have to be comfortable with being uncomfortable.

95. Learn to say, "no."

96. Be direct with respect.

97. Don't let your past pollute your
present or prevent your future.

98. Live a purposed legacy.

99. Be mentally tough.

100. In communicating, tone is strategy.

101. If you don't stand up for yourself, who will?

102. Behavior not addressed will continue.

103. Be willing to let go of one dream for another.

104. Most people aim at nothing in life
and hit it amazingly well.

105. There is a cost to ignorance.

106. Other's opinion of you does not have to become your truth.

107. If you want a different result, you'll have to do something different.

108. "You only have to improve 1% a day to double your effectiveness in 70 days. Find your 1%.

109. Examine what you tolerate and what you accommodate.

110. Take initiative. Be an action
person.

111. Be resourceful.

112. It is difficult to solve a problem at the same level of thinking at which you arrived at it.

113. Your professionalism is greatly
undermined when you make things
personal or take things personal that are
not.

114. Become an expert at reading people.

115. You are your greatest asset!

116. Most people want all the goodies in life with very little effort.

117.   Persistence trumps talent.

118. Create habits that produce desired results.

119. Successful people do what
unsuccessful people are unwilling to do.

120. You've got to have your own sense of direction.

121.   What you are doing today is building your tomorrow.

122. Be authentic.

123. Practice humility.

124. You will act on what you believe to be true – whether it is true or not.

125. Everyone functions in his or her own reality.

126. Be a results person

.

127. You must practice active, strategic career management.

128. Any behavior in a certain context is
useful.

128. "Live full, die empty." Les Brown

To find out about other books and audios by JoAnn R. Corley, go to www.joanncorley.com

To order multiple copies of this book with discount considerations go the
www.joanncorley.com

To bring Ms. Corley to your organization for an onsite seminar, workshop, or keynote – go to www.joanncorley.com